A Time
for Integrity

A Challenge and an Opportunity for each Member of the US Congress

By C. Dudley Bourne

ISBN-13: 978-1496134370

ISBN-10: 1496134370

This book is dedicated to my wife Janet.

Table of Contents

Foreword

This book is focused on examining questionable practices and ethical issues involving Members of the US Congress. It is not about the political issues of the day, such as the Affordable Care Act, immigration, tax reform, or foreign affairs. Nor is it about the processes and procedures, such as cloture votes, filibusters, or partial government shutdowns.

This book is about the failure to act responsibly or ethically by each of the Members of both Houses of the US Congress. It attempts to describe or reference many of these failures and offers solutions, or partial solutions, to some of them.

Chapter 1

Congress:

Low Poll Numbers, But They Get Re-elected Anyway

An apparent contradiction, often noted these days, is that the US Congress has a very low approval rating but continues to have most incumbents re-elected. One reason might be that the Member is doing a good job in representing his district or state and has positions similar to his constituents regarding the role of the federal government and on specific political issues of the day.

If that were the whole story, it would pretty much be an example of representative democracy at its best. But what really influences the re-election of a Member of Congress? Some of the main factors are:

- Gerrymandering, which is discussed in Chapter 4, often provides an extreme advantage to the incumbent.
- Incumbents have large staffs and travel budgets, which have the purpose of assisting them in their lawmaker duties, but which are used extensively for campaigning.

- The franking privilege (taxpayer-funded mailings to constituents), which was intended to keep the public generally informed of issues and activities in Washington, is used simply for campaign literature by each Member. The amount of mailings during the campaign season in election years is far larger than during off-election years.
- Most importantly, the incumbent has far greater access to campaign funds than does the challenger. Most of the campaign funds of the incumbent come from sources in Washington, DC, rather than from his state or district. There is nothing fundamentally wrong about individuals and organizations providing money to a candidate's campaign, or to promoting their positions on certain issues; these are their First Amendment rights of free speech. The problem occurs when Members of Congress engage in unethical behavior in obtaining and using these funds.

The result of these incumbent advantages is that there are very few competitive races. Consider this excerpt from a report from Bloomberg: [1]

> Ninety percent of House members and 91 percent of senators who sought re-election in 2012 were successful, exceeding the incumbent re-election rates of 2010, when 85 percent of

House members and 84 percent of senators seeking re-election were successful. For senators, this year's re-election percentage was the highest since 2004. Low approval ratings have been typically tied to high congressional turnover, but nine in 10 members of Congress won their re-election bids in 2012 with a pre-election approval rating of 21 percent.

According to the University of Virginia Center for Politics, of the 435 seats in the House up for election in 2014, only 43 seats are considered to be either toss-ups or only "leaning" to a specific candidate. Of the remaining 392 seats, 21 are considered to be "likely" wins for the incumbent and the remaining 371 are considered to be completely safe for the incumbent. [2]

So, is it so bad that incumbents win so often? It is, because the current Members of the US Congress have allowed it to become rife with cronyism and corruption.

Chapter 2

Do Your Senators and Your Representative

Deserve Your Vote?

Our representative democracy is a great system of government, perhaps one of the best ever established. But it is certainly not perfect. Throughout our nation's history, we have endured occasional scandals and corruption involving legislators and other public officials at all levels of government. Regretfully, both houses of our US Congress now seem to be failing in meeting their responsibilities, resulting in inefficiency, partisanship, extortion, cronyism, and corruption.

These conditions are best described in two recent books by Mr. Peter Schweizer:

> ***Throw Them All Out*** *- How Politicians and their Friends Get Rich Off Insider Stock Tips, Land Deals, and Cronyism that would send the Rest of Us to Prison*

> ***Extortion*** *- How Politicians Extract Your Money, Buy Votes, and Line Their Own Pockets*

These excellent, well-documented books expose a variety of ethical issues and propose some solutions and improvements. They have provided both motivation and some of the information for the writing of this book. Although the above books speak to issues in both the US Congress and the Executive Branch of the Federal Government, this book is limited to issues and proposed solutions in Congress only.

The examples described and referenced in this book make a strong argument that the longer a Member of Congress serves, the more susceptible he seems to be to cronyism and corruption.

Why? How did we get to this point?

Is this because we are poor judges of our candidates and are simply fooled by smooth salesmen, disguised as statesmen, who have hidden ambitions to go to Washington and get rich through corruption? No. The fact is, representative democracy works. We do select some of the best individuals among us as representatives, although certainly none are perfect.

But the inclination to succumb to the influences of the politics of Washington is great.

Most Members establish homes in the Washington, DC area, while maintaining residences in their district or state. As they continue to be re-elected, Washington becomes more and more their de facto home, where they are most of the time, where most of their friends are, where their children go to school, etc. This is to be expected. But it also means that each Member is gradually influenced less by his district and more and more by the Washington culture.

They become members of the "Permanent Political Class", an accurately descriptive phrase used by Peter Schweizer. They are under pressure to accept the methods by both the Democratic and Republican Parties, regardless of how questionable they may be, and to take advantage of any opportunities available to be re-elected, and to increase their power and influence. Many of these opportunities are unethical but legal. They are legal, of course, because Congress makes the laws and holds itself to a lower standard than the rest of us.

Even after his tenure in Congress, the Member is likely to find continuing work within the Washington power culture.

Each election, a few members of Congress are defeated in their bid for re-election or choose to voluntarily leave office. The 2012 elections saw fewer members leave office than left after 2010, but many of them are already landing in a lobbying firm on K Street.

From the book **This Town**, by Mark Leibovich [3], a witty and enlightening view of the Washington DC culture:

> *Calculations vary on how many former members of Congress have joined the influence-peddling set. By the middle of 2011, at least 160 former law-makers were working as lobbyists in Washington, according to First Street, a website that tracks lobbying trends in D.C., in April 2013. The Center for Responsive*

Politics listed 412 former members who are influence peddling, 305 of whom are registered as federal lobbyists. Hundreds more were reaping huge, often six- and seven- figure salaries as consultants or "senior advisors," those being among the noms de choice for avoiding the scarlet L.

Mr. Leibovich also provides this description of a typical transition for a Member from office to the lobbying world: [4]

Republican Senator Robert Bennett and another retiring Senator, Byron Dorgan, Democrat of North Dakota, announced on the same day that they would be joining Arent Fox, a major downtown law firm that includes a large lobbying component. Both Bennett and Dorgan had served on the Senate Committee on Appropriations, which gave them vast knowledge of how Congress allocates cash. It also made them coveted recruits for K-Street.

Technically, former senators are forbidden from lobbying their old colleagues by a two-year "cooling off period", so Bennett and Dorgan joined "Arent Fox as "senior policy advisors" in the government relations department. There is little practical difference in what a former officeholder who lobbies does and what a former officeholder who "senior advises" does.

For instance, someone like Dorgan could correctly say he has not formally registered to lobby even though he owns the title of co-chair of the firm's government relations practice. In other words, he essentially oversees a staff of lobbyists. He talks all the time to his former law-making colleagues, and he can also use his specialized knowledge and access to call on old colleagues, friends, and fund-raisers to advance his client's interests in bending a law or provision to their favor. He knows not only whom to call but also the phone number and who hired the staffer and precisely what to say to make things "happen".

While in the Senate, Dorgan was often quick to get all contemptuously righteous about people on the Hill cashing in on their public service. When Jack Abramoff testified before the Senate Committee on Indian Affairs, Dorgan beat him up over the "cesspool of greed" that surrounded Abramoff's lobbying practice. In his subsequent memoir, Abramoff wrote of Dorgan, "I guess it wasn't a cesspool when he had his hand out to take over $75,000 in campaign contributions from our team and clients". (The Washington Post reported in 2005 that Dorgan said he would return $67,000 in donations from Indian tribes that Abramoff represented.)

So, what are some of the specific corrupt practices in Congress? This book groups these practices into four categories (with some overlapping points among the categories). Each group is described in later chapters, along with proposed solutions:

- Earmarks and other similar methods of applying specific funds for particular projects or industries to unrelated bills
- Gerrymandering of congressional districts
- Extortion and misuse of campaign funds
- Insider trading by Members of Congress

Chapter 3

Earmarks and other similar methods of applying specific funds to bills for particular projects or industries

But wait....haven't earmarks been outlawed by Congress?

Well, sort of...both Houses have continued a moratorium on earmarks through the end of the 113th Congress (to the end of 2014). But whether earmarks are stopped permanently is an open question. They may be reinstated for the next Congress and, in any event, some groups worry that much of the same activity may have just gone underground.

This subject should be considered more broadly, including not just the earmarks that are now on hold, but in the context of all situations in which a congressional bill includes specific funding that is unrelated to it. The following table offers some general categories.

The Practice of Applying Funds for Specific Purposes into a Bill – A general, unofficial spectrum

General Description	Comments
An earmark applied by a Member who directly benefits from it. Examples would be an earmark for a project that directly affects the value of real estate, stock, or other assets that the member owns. A variation of this occurs when a Member places an earmark that directly benefits *another* Member, as a favor to be collected later.	This is simply criminal. Against the rules in both Houses. Members have on occasion been punished for these activities. But the standard is too low. From **Throw Them All Out**: "Any Member of Congress…can quietly insert an earmark into any big bill in order to widen the road in front of their house. As long as one other person lives on that road, the ethics committee will sign off on it."[5]
An earmark applied by a Member that directly benefits a company, when the primary owners or investors in that company are the Member's family, relatives, business associates, or political supporters.	Unethical, but not illegal by the Ethics Committee standards. Peter Schweizer provides many examples of earmarks in this category and the above category in his book, **Throw Them All Out.** [6]
Any earmark, regardless of its worth or cost, if a Member is allowed to place it primarily in exchange for his vote on the bill to which it is attached.	Counterproductive and unethical. This occurs routinely and overtly in both Houses. Many people defend this practice as necessary to make our government function. This is nonsense.

An earmark that supports a non-essential project in the Members's district that specifies particular companies or groups, without any competitive processes, and that is funded primarily because of the Members status in Congress.	This unethical practice also occurs frequently in both Houses. Funds to use for earmarks are routinely assigned to each member, with higher ranking members receiving the most.
Unneeded programs - defense systems, contracts, not wanted by the DoD or other agency	Uninformed and wasteful. In the DoD example, a specific weapons system or component should be purchased only if it accomplishes a certain mission better than other competitive systems and is a priority compared to many other possible acquisitions. In an earmark, the Member simply requires the purchase of whatever product or service offered by the contractor in his district or state, or that has provided sufficient campaign funds.
Large funding items inserted into an unrelated bill, primarily as a political strategy to try to humiliate the opposing party. For example, including "funding the troops" in an unrelated bill.	Distasteful, a waste of time, and becoming very trite. Not an "earmark" in the strict definition of the word, but still an outrage. Both Democrats and Republicans do this, mostly to manufacture talking points for the media.

On March 19, 2012, CREW (Citizens for Responsibility and Ethics in Washington) published the 2012 Family Affair report [7], after examining the records of all 435 members of the House. One of its findings were that 38 members (24 Democrats and 14 Republicans) earmarked to a family business, employer, or associated nonprofit.

But there are many who support earmarks, and hail them as necessary for a functioning government. An editorial in Forbes by Rick Ungar, "Why Congress Cannot Operate Without The Bribing Power Of Earmarks" [8], makes that case:

> *For starters, if you believe we have done away with the concept of earmarking money for special projects back home—think again. The earmark moratorium has brought forward an even more insidious process called "lettermarking" where Congressional slush funds are created as tools for funding pet projects without even the limited accountability and public information that came with earmarking. While earmarks required publication of a pork project—along with the amount of taxpayer money being spent and identification of the elected official proposing the earmark— lettermarking allows for such expenditures without any identification of the project, sum and sponsoring legislator whatsoever...*

The moratorium on earmarks went into existence in February 2011. Since that time we have seen some of the greatest legislative fails in the history of the nation, highlighted by the debt ceiling fiasco of 2011, the inability to pass a jobs bill, an ever-increasing vacancy rate in the federal judiciary as one nominee after another is shelved and, of course, the current fiscal cliff clunker that might be the most embarrassing and damaging display of congressional incompetence of all.

One cannot help but wonder if our current inability to legislate our way out of a paper bag might be different were party leaders and the President to, once again, be free to avail themselves of the one thing that could always win the hearts and minds of elected officials who care, first and foremost, for their own jobs—a healthy and legal bribe....

Cynical? Absolutely.

But how is it any more cynical than a political system that welcomes the bribery offered up by special interests in the guise of huge and often unlimited campaign contributions that benefit incumbents in exchange for their vote— particularly if the cost of earmarks to the taxpayer is far less than the cost to taxpayers when our legislators refuse to act, despite knowing that their inaction will cost our economy, and therefore our taxpayers, even more money?

Mr. Unger certainly makes an important point in his description of the earmark system simply going underground through the use of "lettermarking." But do we really have to choose between one type of dysfunction and another? We sent representatives to Congress to deliberate and act on matters of public policy. If some of them have no motivation to do so without getting earmarks, then the answer is not to reinstate earmarks, but to vote out those Congressmen.

But Mr. Unger is not alone in his views. From a Roll Call article by Humberto Sanchez [9]:

> *Though the bans have passed with little public opposition, Sen. Lamar Alexander said he hopes earmarks will be brought back in the future. "Earmarks became a scandal and we needed to clean them up," the Tennessee Republican said Monday evening. "But it's time for us to begin to think about our constitutional responsibilities, which are to appropriate dollars." Alexander noted that he voted for the moratorium again this year.*
>
> *Other longtime GOP supporters of earmarks include Sen. Lisa Murkowski of Alaska, who*

serves on the Appropriations Committee. She told Alaska Public Radio Network that she doesn't agree with the strategy.

Yes, it is the constitutional responsibility of Congress to appropriate dollars, but as a federal budget, not as a bunch of pet projects whose main purpose is to help get the incumbent re-elected.

Since the temporary moratorium on earmarks, alternate strategies called "letter-marking and "phone-marking" are being used.   These need to be discouraged or banned.   This editorial from The Hill gives insight into these developments: [10]

Lobbyists already hamstrung by the earmark bans in Congress could be marginalized even more if the Obama administration approves a draft memo that would require agencies to disclose lawmakers' requests for federal funds.

Earmark bans have been instituted in the House and Senate this year, but the moratorium on the practice has not prevented lawmakers from seeking federal funds for favored projects.

Lawmakers often contact federal agencies directly in an attempt to influence where money is spent, a practice often dubbed "letter-marking" or "phone-marking."

The messages from members of Congress are not typically made public, though the press sometimes obtains them through Freedom of Information Act requests. Several lawmakers have been embarrassed when their letters asking for federal funds were disclosed under FOIA, undercutting their stated positions of wanting to cut government spending.

The draft memo from the Obama administration could make disclosure of letter-marking and phone-marking routine — a possibility welcomed by watchdog groups, but feared by lobbyists who make their living off the appropriations process.

Steve Ellis, vice president of the budget watchdog group Taxpayers for Common Sense, praised the administration's plan and said there is no reason for the requests to be kept secret.

"If a lawmaker or staff wants to make their opinion known to the executive branch about this, that or the other project or provision, then they should stand by that opinion and make it known," Ellis told The Hill.

"The fight against parochial, special-interest spending is one that we are winning

incrementally. I don't care if lawmakers are less likely to write if they were disclosed, because then I'm sure they shouldn't have been writing them in the first place," Ellis said.

The National Journal reported Sunday that the Obama administration has begun to circulate a memo on Capitol Hill that would have all federal agencies release letters from lawmakers that direct agency officials what projects to fund.

"Too often, federal agencies are pressured informally to show special favor to certain parties or interests in the course of agency decisionmaking concerning federal projects, programs, contracts, and grants. Like legislated earmarks, these pressures on agency decisionmaking also undermine the neutral application of merit-based and competitive criteria for the allocation of federal resources," the memo states, according to the National Journal.

As various earmark bans have taken hold in recent years, K Street has adapted by mastering the competitive grant system used for federal funds. One technique that has been used by lobbyists is to have a lawmaker vouch for their client's project in a letter to the funding agency, especially if the project would benefit the lawmaker's constituents.

Under the draft memo, those letters would be disclosed and searchable on the Internet within 30 days of their receipt by the agency. That might make lawmakers shy about defending various projects.

"It will make members of Congress and their staff think twice about writing letters, making calls, holding meetings with federal agencies where pending grants, loans, contracts or cooperative agreements are being decided," said one appropriations lobbyist.

The lobbyist compared the draft memo to the restrictions the administration placed on lobbyists when it came to stimulus funds. Those rules led several agency officials to minimize or avoid all contact with K Street as they worked to implement the economic recovery package.

Press reports have suggested lettermarking is still used by lawmakers, and the practice has likely become more prevalent because of the earmark ban.

"The moratorium has certainly reduced the practice of earmarks, but it is easily sidestepped through letter-marking and phone-marking practices, which appear to be fairly common, but no one really knows for sure because these are not publicly disclosed," said Craig Holman, government affairs lobbyist for Public Citizen.

Holman noted the draft memo builds on an executive order by President George W. Bush that ordered agencies not to accept lawmakers' funding requests unless they were authorized by legislation passed by Congress. Holman said that he feels that the order has been ignored by the agencies, so he hopes Obama is more aggressive with ensuring compliance with the draft memo.

Others are worried that the draft memo would center more of the government's spending power in the executive branch, rather than on Capitol Hill.

Howard Marlowe, president of the American League of Lobbyists, said his group is concerned that if the memo were issued, it would lead to constituents not asking for congressional help.

"What concerns the American League of Lobbyists about this proposal is its potential to deter constituents from asking their federal-elected officials to support their needs. That is the right of every American that is guaranteed by the Constitution," Marlowe said.

The above article was published in November 2011, but letter-marking continues, as shown in a September 2013 article: [11]

According to Taxpayers for Common Sense, a nonpartisan budget watchdog, lawmakers have worked out an end run.

In a practice called "letter-marking," they now write executive branch officials asking them to fund their pet projects. Or they beseech them through phone calls — or "phone-marking." According to Steve Ellis, vice president of the group, legislators may even set aside slush funds in laws they pass to accommodate requests they plan to make of various agencies.

Such requests, he concedes, are not as powerful as earmarks, which were included in law. And, agency heads aren't required to listen — although if a member is powerful enough, like Barbara Mikulski, D-Md., who chairs the Senate

Appropriations Committee, they are likely to pay heed ($126.8 million in 2010).

But such requests occur in the dark. As Ellis points out, "They are a lot less traceable than earmarks." They are not public. To see letter-marks, you have to file a Freedom of Information Act (FOIA) request with a particular federal agency. According to Josh Israel, an investigator who's dug into the matter for the Center for American Progress, a left-leaning think tank, agencies may take months to respond. When the letter-marks come, they are redacted...

...in 2011, the Obama administration began to consider a proposal to require federal departments and agencies to make such letters public in a searchable database. So far, no results on that front.

Some comments:

The executive order by President George W. Bush that ordered agencies not to accept lawmakers' funding requests unless they were authorized by legislation passed by Congress should be enforced.

The Obama administration needs to make letter-marking requests available to the public in a searchable database, as planned.

Regarding Howard Marlowe's comments in the above article from The Hill, it is simply incorrect that these practices are a constitutional right. Certainly any American can talk with his senator or representative about anything – that is obvious free speech. But no American has a constitutional right to receive special treatment as a result of efforts by his congressman.

More earmark support comes from the book **Cheese Factories on the Moon – Why Earmarks Are Good for American Democracy** by Scott A. Frisch and Sean Q. Kelly. They provide detailed insight into how the earmark system works and offer some defenses for it. From the Preface: [12]

> *We do not claim that all earmarks are wise uses of government dollars, nor do we assert that the earmark process is completely free of corruption. However, on balance we believe that the current earmark process plays a useful role in the American system of government and is typically more open to public scrutiny than alternative methods of spending taxpayer dollars. This book is an argument; it is not unbiased. We intend to be provocative by turning a critical eye on the typical arguments made against earmarks.*

In that same spirit, this book will take issue with some of the points that they offer.

Their general position supporting earmarks (paraphrased) is that a Member who knows the needs of his state or district can do a better job of selecting and funding projects than a "faceless bureaucrat" in the Executive Branch with a "one size fits all" perspective.

On page 42, they offer a perspective from former Senator Trent Lott:

> *Senator Trent Lott, who served as the Senate Republican leader for several years, suggested that it (placing earmarks) was part of the difficult process of leading that institution, which he referred to "herding cats." Using earmarks was part of the process and "there's nothing sinister about that." Not all legislation is responsive to the needs of all constituents at all times; there may be things about a bill that may be the general interest but the bill does not necessarily serve the interest of a subset of American voters. Says Lott, "These men and women come to the Senate to represent their constituents; sometimes they can't do it in a way they feel is needed, and then at some point their vote becomes critical and you try to find a way to accommodate them." Earmarks become the means by which a leader can entice a legislator to swallow a bitter legislative pill. As*

House Whip, Lott explained, he encouraged members to come to him on a regular basis, but he discouraged members from approaching him when their vote was needed; he wanted to avoid the appearance of a quid pro quo arrangement. [13]

It is difficult to understand how this is a defense of earmarks. Former Senator Lott clearly explains (as have many others) that the earmark is accepted from the Member so that the Member will vote on the bill it is attached to, which is on an entirely different subject.

It is the duty of each Member to vote for or against each bill based upon its merits, not on whether a side deal is made. The main problem is not about the money, but about the fact that our legislative process, which has the goal of setting just laws and sound public policy, is being hijacked.

On page 83, Frisch and Kelly offer this:

The founders thus invested in Congress considerable power, including the power of the purse, which would allow the legislature to resist the incursions of the executive into the legislative realm; they also intended to place the spending power close to the sovereign people. ...By using earmarks, the Congress has pressed the Executive Branch to pursue programs and technologies that have otherwise gone unrecognized by the executive bureaucracy. Critics of earmarks argue that spending decisions based upon objective criteria are better suited for determining expenditures. But we demonstrate that program managers can steer contracts toward particular vendors, and they do so regularly outside of the watchful eye of the media, watchdog groups, and the public. Arguments that support shifting the power of the purse further into the executive branch would undermine the delicate balance developed by the framers. As we argue, giving the executive branch additional power to determine spending would shift power to unelected bureaucrats who are not democratically accountable. The federal bureaucracy is famously opaque; the potential for corruption in the executive bureaucracy is enormous.

Some responses:

Certainly the power of the purse resides with Congress, which is why it is required by the Constitution to establish an annual budget. But it hasn't in five years. Instead it is being suggested that if only Members of Congress can be allowed to create enough earmarks (which total less than 1% of annual federal spending), they must be doing their jobs. How about trying to manage the other 99%?

Acquisition executives in the executive branch are under the watchful eye of the media, watchdog groups, and the public just as much as Congress is, but neither is scrutinized enough.

If unelected bureaucrats in the executive branch (also known as senior executives, who are career professionals, not political appointees) decide to circumvent the acquisition process by steering contracts toward particular vendors, they do so at their peril. That is against all acquisition regulations. In contrast, members of Congress routinely place earmarks for specific vendors, and brag about it. From a CREW report (Citizens for Responsibility and Ethics in Washington; Top Scandals of 2012): [14]

> *Members of Congress so concerned about the fiscal cliff and wasteful government spending don't apply the same standards to their own spending decisions. For instance, House Appropriations Chairman Hal Rogers (R-KY) forced the Army to pay at least $17 million for overpriced helicopter drip pans made by a Kentucky company, the employees of which just so happened to be major donors to his campaigns.*

This is a book about corruption, not budgets and taxes. But, when the primary argument in favor of earmarks is that, yes, it is somewhat corrupt, but the representative knows the local needs better than a "faceless bureaucrat", who is also inefficient and maybe corrupt, then one response has to be: then why send that money to Washington in the first place? As has been said before: Is this round trip necessary? Can't the locals, who are asking for the earmark and jumping through the hoops with the representatives and the lobbyists, make a more sound and efficient local investment on their own without even going to Washington? Wouldn't THAT "place the spending power close to the sovereign people"?

Congress has the responsibility to provide an annual federal budget, with top line funding for each department of the Executive Branch. There are twelve appropriations bills which need to be passed each year:

- Agriculture, Rural Development, and Food and Drug Administration
- Commerce, Justice, and Science
- Defense
- Energy and Water Development
- Financial Services and General Government (includes judicial branch, the Executive Office of the President, and District of Columbia appropriations)
- Homeland Security

- Interior and Environment
- Labor, Health and Human Services, and Education
- Legislative Branch
- Military Construction and Veterans Affairs
- State and Foreign Operations
- Transportation and Housing and Urban Development

Then each department in the Executive Branch executes its responsibilities within its appropriated budget. When goods or services need to be purchased, they should use the proper, in-place, acquisition processes with competitive source selections. It is never appropriate for Congress to pass an appropriations bill for any of the above departments that includes an earmark or any other specific spending requirement.

We should make the ban on earmarks permanent. We should adopt the requirement to make public all funding requests by Members of Congress (through "letter-marking" or "phone-marking") to executive branch officials. We should strengthen the rules for FOIA requests made to Members of Congress, to prevent delays and redactions. There are rarely national security issues involved in these requests, and no reason for them to be hidden.

Beyond that, Peter Schweizer offers a common-sense reform: [15]

> We should adopt a single-subject rule for all bills. Article III of the Florida Constitution "requires that every law shall embrace but one subject and matter properly connected therewith." In other words, each bill needs to be focused on one specific subject. You shouldn't be able to slip something in on an unrelated subject.

Chapter 4

Gerrymandering:

A Roadblock to Effective Democracy and

a National Embarrassment

The practice of establishing ridiculous, embarrassing congressional districts is an old, trite story. That doesn't make it any less important or less shameful. Here is some background from the Brennan Center for Justice: [16]

> ***What is redistricting?*** *Members of Congress, state legislators, and many county and municipal offices are elected by voters grouped into districts. At least once per decade, usually after a Census, district lines are redrawn, block by block. Populations change. Some districts gain residents, some lose them. Some districts increase the numbers of minorities, some districts lose them. District boundaries are redrawn to ensure each district has about the same number of people and to fulfill the constitutional guarantee that each voter has an equal say. Based on the 2010 census, each Congressional district has an average*

population of about 711,000, which is nearly a 10 percent increase from the 2000 census, when each district had an average of 647,000 people. In 2010, some states lost congressional seats and others gained them. For example, Texas gained four districts and New York lost two.

Who draws the lines? *Each state decides. In most states, the line drawers are politicians along with hired consultants. Often, state legislators draw the map, which the governor can veto. Some states have special commissions that advise legislators on drawing the map, or that serve as backup mapmakers if the legislature deadlocks. A few states have independent commissions so politicians and public officials cannot directly draw their own districts. Some states try to prevent a single political party from controlling the process. Some do not, providing one party a major advantage if it controls the state legislature. In other states, politicians from both parties simply work together to draw districts that often protect incumbents.*

Why does redistricting matter? *Redistricting affects political power. It determines which party controls Congress and state and local governments across the country. Even when the* *population is divided equally, drawing the lines one way can reward Democrats and punish Republicans or vice versa. Some line-drawing can protect incumbents. Some line-drawing can guarantee they will face a potent challenger, either from their own party or the opposite party. Consequently, redistricting has a direct bearing on what matters a legislature chooses to tackle, and which to ignore.*

How should the lines be drawn? *A good redistricting process should help a community secure meaningful representation. Other than meeting the constitutional requirement that all votes should count equally, there is no magic formula. Many states consider "communities of interest" when drawing their districts. That's just a term for groups of people who share common social, cultural, racial, economic, geographic, or other concerns. These groups are likely to have similar legislative interests as well, and that means they can benefit from common representation in the government. This goes much deeper than Republican or Democrat. A district of farmers, say, and a district of city dwellers will probably elect representatives that reflect differing histories, priorities, and aspirations. Other redistricting goals — like keeping a district compact or within county borders — are usually proxies for* *keeping communities intact. A good redistricting process will be open and transparent, allowing communities to ask questions and give input. This participation is important, since communities are the basic units of well-designed districts.*

What is gerrymandering? *Gerrymandering refers to the manipulation of district lines to protect or change political power. Any change in district lines affects politics. But a gerrymander is a deliberate and, according to opponents, unfair attempt to draw district lines to increase the likelihood of a particular political result. Incumbents, for example, have an incentive to create districts that are likely to re-elect them, sometimes dividing communities among one or more districts when a single district containing the entire community would better represent their interests.*

The following is an excerpt from a 2005, but still very relevant, study from The Cato Institute: [17]

Partisan gerrymanders are very effective in increasing a party's share of legislative seats. The creation of so-called safe districts allows the two major parties to work together to minimize their respective election risks. The minority party usually prefers a level of certainty regarding its base number of legislative seats. To the extent that political parties cooperate and compromise with each other, the redistricting process has degenerated into a conspiracy against competitive elections, undermining the fundamental notion of representation. This anti-competitive trend led economist Randall Holcombe to conclude that "political markets are divided in the same way that cartels would divide markets in order to make each member a monopolist in his own territory to help enforce the cartel agreement." In many states, gerrymandering may be a more serious problem today than it has ever been in American history. Representative democracy is a system of government whereby citizens control the government through their chosen representatives. In the United States, however, political representatives increasingly choose those they will represent, as election results tend to be predetermined by gerrymandering. Even politicians such as Tom Davis (R-VA) say that it used to be the voters who chose the politicians. Now the politicians choose the voters. Therefore, redistricting has important consequences for the health of the American political system. Under a system of gerrymandered districts, the health of American democracy is at risk. Gerrymandering diminishes voter sovereignty over elections.

Partisan legislative gerrymandering severely undermines electoral competitiveness, arguably to the point of violating the Constitution's Equal Protection Clause, as it consigns electoral majorities to minority status on the basis of their political views.

Maybe the easiest way to understand the extent of this problem is simply to review some current congressional district maps. Three of the most egregious examples are shown here.

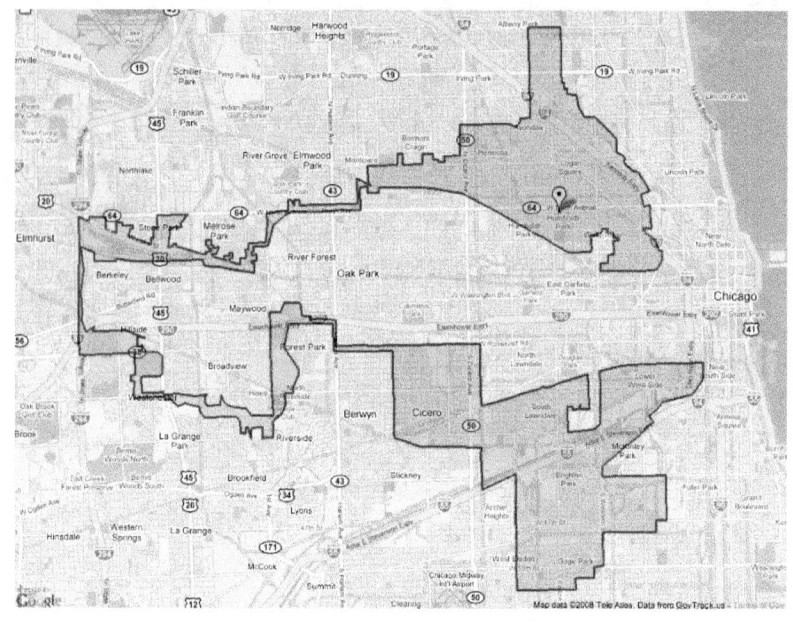

Illinois Congressional District Number 4

Pennsylvania Congressional District Number 7

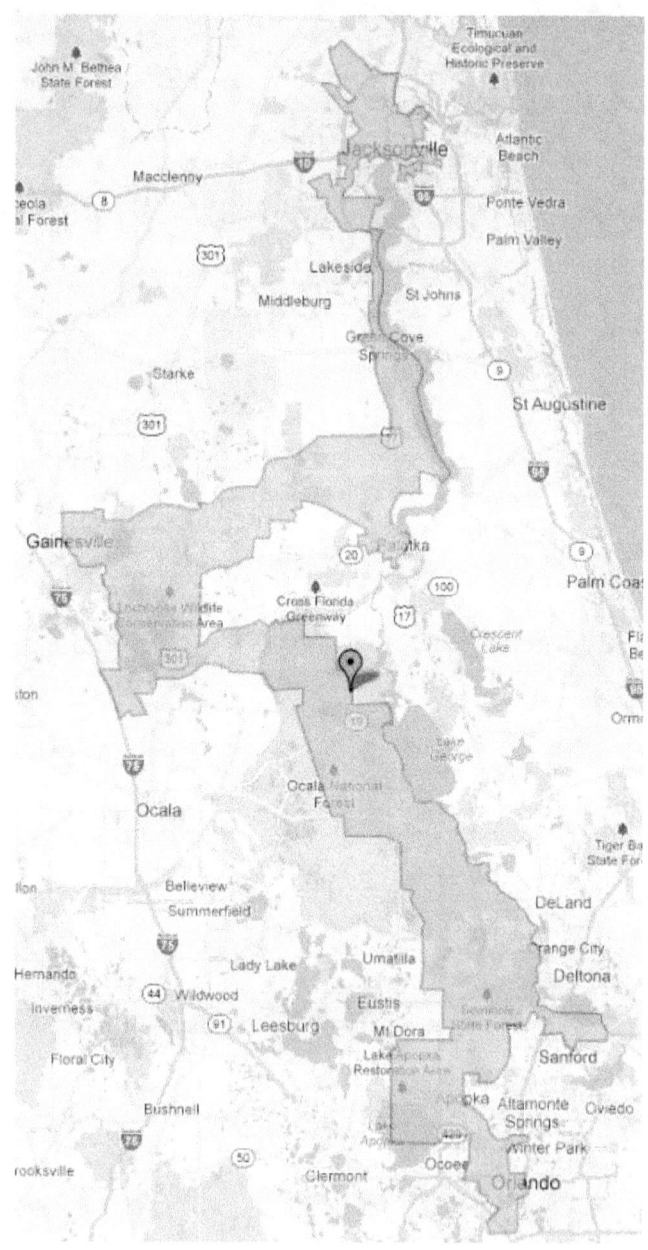

Florida Congressional District Number 5

But how is the US Congress at fault for this gerrymandering; isn't each state legislature responsible for redistricting? Yes, but let's not be gullible. Each state legislature is very influenced by its Members of the US Congress. Any state will of course attempt to accomplish redistricting to the advantage of the political party that controls the state legislature at the time of the census. But, beyond that, the two parties often work together, as suggested earlier, to protect and support the incumbents of both parties.

The ways that politicians manipulate districts are so well-known that political insiders have a special gerrymandering vocabulary: Politicians can "pack" certain communities into a single district, "bleach" out minorities, "crack" troublesome voting blocks between different districts, "kidnap" a troublesome representative by putting his or her house in a separate district from his or her former constituents, or "hijack" a district by redrawing the lines to pit two incumbents from the same party against each other. [18]

These practices are not in the best interests of anyone except the specific political parties and/or incumbents at the time.

So, what are some solutions? First, we should recognize constructive efforts that have already been made and safeguards that are now in place:

Some state legislatures now use independent commissions to execute the redistricting, while others have non-partisan staffs propose maps for state legislature approval, as shown here:

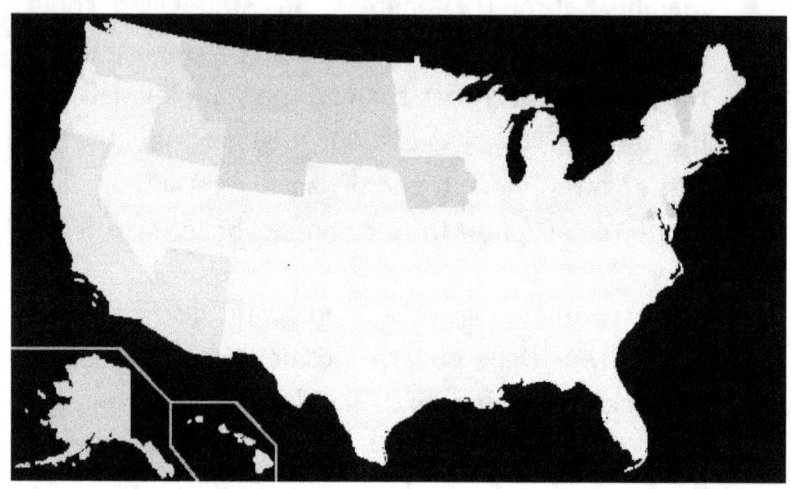

Redistricting Methods by State after the 2010 census.

State commissions control redistricting in Washington, Idaho, California, Hawaii, and Arizona.

In Iowa, non-partisan staff proposes the map, but the state legislature votes on the proposal.

Alaska, Delaware, Montana, North Dakota, South Dakota, Vermont, and Wyoming have only one representative.

Legislatures control redistricting in the remaining states.

When state legislatures consider inputs from the residents of the state (through communications between interest groups and the state legislators, public meetings, etc.) more than they consider influence from their current incumbents of the US Congress, redistricting will almost certainly be improved. The process in which state legislatures have the responsibility and power to accomplish the redistricting is not an inherently flawed concept. Someone has to do it, and elections have consequences.

The US Supreme Court has made rulings on redistricting, but has properly been somewhat restrained in deference to the separation of powers clause.

The US Executive Branch also has some jurisdiction with regard to redistricting through the Voting Rights Act.

So, considering the above, what further should be done to eliminate or reduce extreme gerrymandering? It is an important, complex, and fundamental issue that won't be completely solved anytime soon, certainly not within these pages.

But, it has been noted that the more compact that a district is, the less likely it is gerrymandered for partisan advantage. There have been court rulings that require that a district be compact, but no specific standard has been established. Various studies have been done and various mathematical algorithms have been proposed as a way to set a standard.

This concept seems to be a powerful tool to stop extreme gerrymandering. It won't prevent gerrymandering, but it can significantly restrain it. Here is a suggested technique and some examples:

Standard: The ratio of the length of the perimeter of a district, squared, and then divided by the area of that district, must be less than 60.

$$\text{(length of perimeter)}^2 / \text{(area)} = \text{less than 60}$$

Examples: Circle (most compact area) = 12.56

               Square = 16

               Rectangle with sides of 1 and 6 = 32.67

States that have only one US representative would obviously be exempt from this ratio requirement.

The following are examples of some of districts with the ratio for each.

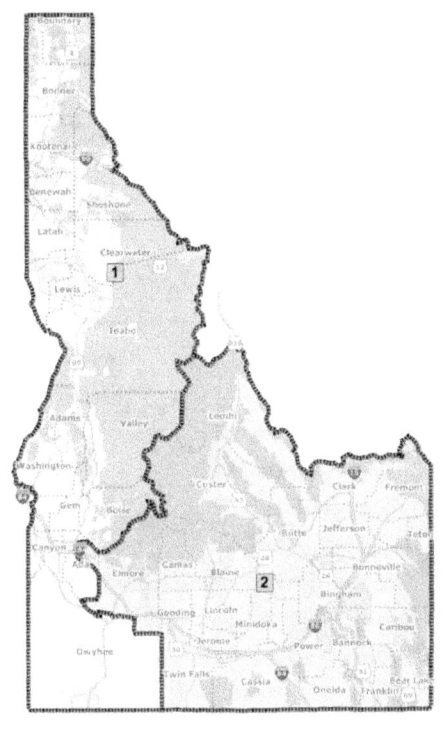

Idaho Congressional Districts

Ratio for District 1 is only 45.9, although it includes the panhandle. Ratio for District 2 is only 23.8.

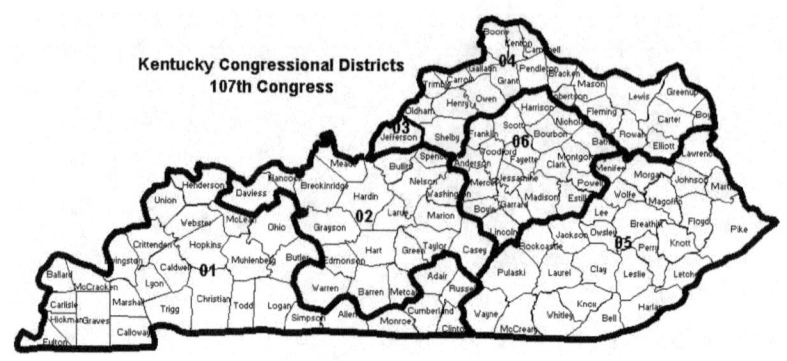

Kentucky Congressional Districts
107th Congress

Kentucky Congressional Districts

District	Ratio
1	81.5
2	88.3
3	22.1
4	99.3
5	32.4
6	38.3

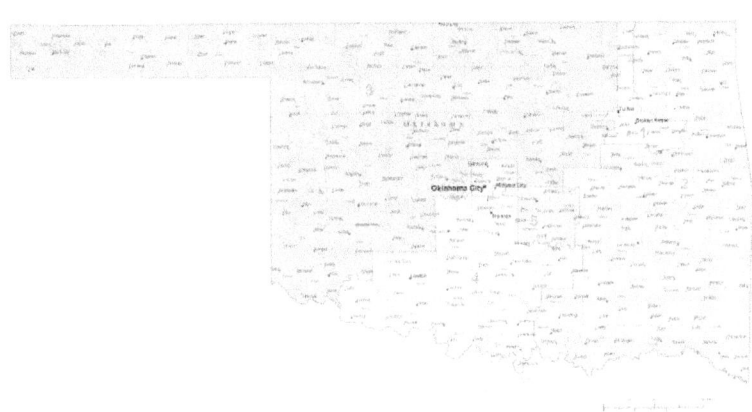

Oklahoma Congressional Districts

The ratio for District 3 is 44.0, even though the Oklahoma panhandle forces it to be less compact than it would be otherwise.

District	Ratio
1	61.5
2	31.7
3	44.0
4	33.1
5	34.0

From these examples, it is evident that a congressional district can be shaped to conform to various requirements and still be somewhat compact.

The ratio of 60 suggested here may be too restrictive a standard for compactness; perhaps a maximum allowable ratio of 80 or 100 would be more workable. In any event, this rule would prevent the extreme gerrymandering shown in the first three examples in this chapter. To review, this table shows the ratios for the examples of districts shown in this chapter:

State	District	Ratio
Kentucky	1	81.5
Kentucky	2	88.3
Kentucky	3	22.1
Kentucky	4	99.3
Kentucky	5	32.4
Kentucky	6	38.3
Oklahoma	1	61.5
Oklahoma	2	31.7
Oklahoma	3	44.0
Oklahoma	4	33.1
Oklahoma	5	34.0
Idaho	1	45.9
Idaho	2	23.8
Ratios for the first three examples in this chapter are below:		
Illinois	4	**511.0**
Pennsylvania	7	**165.9**
Florida	5	**218.5**

Let's stop letting incumbents select their own voters, and let's improve on our redistricting process. Let's use this ratio (or something similar) as a standard for required compactness.

Chapter 5

Extortion and misuse of campaign funds

"Sure, I will consider the language that your lobbying firm/ industry wants in this bill….By the way; I am having a fund-raising dinner tomorrow night, would you like to come?"

This is a fictitious quote, but, sadly, it represents a situation that occurs daily in Washington. In the book **Extortion** [19], Peter Schweizer describes how Members of Congress extort money from the private sector, not unlike the "protection money" often demanded by mobsters. From pages 12 and 13:

> *If you are a politician, the key is linking what you do in your official duties to a sophisticated fund-raising apparatus. Washington politicians have direct, detailed, and regular communications between their congressional staffers – who write, analyze, and assess bills, as well as perform constituent services – and their congressional fund-raising teams. This allows politicians and their fund-raisers to target those who might be vulnerable to political extortion. Sometimes you have to wonder: who is more important, the chief of staff or the chief fund-raiser?...*

There's a lexicon for modern political extortion. Politicians from some parts of the country refer to "milker bills", which are intended to "milk" companies and individuals to pass or stop legislation that will benefit or hurt them. Others call them "juicer" bills because they are introduced largely for the purpose of squeezing money out of the target. Some call them "fetcher bills" because they are drafted and introduced to "fetch" lavish and lucrative attention from lobbyists and powerful interests. Whatever you call them, these bills are designed not to make good law, but rather to raise money. The politicians are not necessarily interested in having the bill pass. Often these bills are very narrow in focus and would do little to benefit their constituents.

Indeed, politicians often don't want these bills to pass because if they do, the opportunity for future extortion is removed. A good milker bill can be introduced repeatedly, milking donors year after year. Laws that do pass, especially narrowly focused ones, are purposely designed to expire every few years so politicians can revisit the issue and "juice" the same people. The best kind of all is the "double-milker" or "double-juicer," which is designed to play two deep-pocketed industries against one another, setting off a lucrative arms race. Members of Congress can milk each bill multiple times.

The extortion employed by Members of Congress is deeply embedded in the Washington culture, as described in pages 59-61 of **Extortion**: [20]

> *In the days leading up to the contentious Dodd-Frank financial reform bill vote, Congressman Joseph Crowley, a member of the powerful House Ways and Means Committee, held four fund-raising events targeting financial institutions that stood to gain or lose from the vote. The day before the final vote, Crowley held two fund-raising events, including a cocktail hour hosted at a lobbyist's home. Of the forty-two guests who showed up, thirty-one were lobbyists for the financial reform bill or their coworkers. After cocktails, Crowley then went to a dinner with thirteen other lobbyists who were working on the financial reform bill. The cost to attend was $2,500 for PACs and $1,000 for individuals. Emails from his campaign show that he specifically targeted financial industry lobbyists for donations. Crowley raised $90,000 in one night.*
>
> *The day before the final vote on Dodd-Frank, Congressman Tom Price of Georgia, a member of the Financial Services Committee, solicited donations at a "Financial Services Industry*

Luncheon." It was organized with the input of Bank of America employees, who helped to write the invitation list. All but three of the individuals who attended Price's luncheon were lobbyists for the bill.

Congressman John Campbell of California, also a member of the House Financial Services Committee, asked representatives of several financial institutions – Bank of America, Chubb Corporation, MasterCard, and New York Life – if they wanted one-on-one meetings about the bill. Campbell also held a "Financial Services Dinner" on October 2009, one day before the markup of the bill in committee. Like Price and Crowley, Campbell also held multiple fund-raising events in the days before the final vote.

John Hofmeister, the former president of Shell Oil, recalls, "If you are invited, you are expected to be there. There is an implicit aspect of the request that makes that clear. And when you get there, you better show up with a check."

Hofmeister's description of these events resembles a shakedown. Not much needs to be said, unless you fail to comply. "You are standing in the room, and there is a glass bowl in the center. You are supposed to place your check in that bowl. Someone who works for the politician is watching from the corner to make *sure everyone puts their check in the bowl. If you don't - they are going to come by and ask you why. That is the expectation."*

And if you fail to pay your tithe? Politicians will be very blunt, says Hofmeister. "Why am I meeting with you?" they will ask. "What have you done for me?"

Many executives and corporate PACs do what Hofmeister did — they purposely give to both sides. It's kind of like paying protection money to two rival gangs. "I made it a practice to give to each side equally." He told me. "If you want access or to raise something with them that concerns you, they check to see if you are a donor before they meet with you."

Politicians spend so much time raising money because that is how you win elections. Outspending your opponent is no guarantee, of course. American politics is full of examples of wealthy candidates going down in flames. But the evidence is pretty overwhelming that money matters. Nine out of ten times in the House of Representatives, and eight out of ten times in the Senate, the candidate who spends the most money wins.

Below is an excerpt from a June 2013 Daily Beast commentary [21] that decries this situation involving lobbyists and other powerful industry organizations:

> As lobbyists make their clients' cases to members of Congress, those members certainly know just how much those lobbyists have helped. That help isn't a crime. Indeed, lobbyists are meticulous in keeping their behavior within formal ethical lines. But even within those lines, influence is peddled. And for members starved for campaign funds, even a very little bit can go a long way.
>
> The economy of that dance plainly corrupts Congress. Because rather than staying focused—as Madison promised they would be—"upon the People alone," Congress is increasingly focused upon its funders.
>
> Yet those funders are not America. They are the tiniest slice of America. No more than 1/20th of 1 percent of us give enough to count as a relevant funder of a congressional campaign. And as members spend hours every day frantically trying to find some of that 0.05 percent who might help, they learn the words their funders want to hear.

This book has a slightly different take on this issue. When it works right, lobbyists are a voice of the people. Each lobbyist should present the views and positions of the industry, union, or interest group that he represents. How else will truckers, doctors, school teachers, people supporting particular agendas, etc., have their voices heard when legislation is being considered? How else are the Members of Congress supposed to become informed? (Yes, there are other ways to be heard: voting, town hall meetings, petitions, etc., but the lobbyist has the distinct advantage of being able to provide inputs *at the time the legislation is being written*.) Although the lobbyists may be only 1/20th of 1 percent of the population, they represent many groups and individuals who are simply exerting their First Amendment rights of free speech. The problem, of course, is when it deteriorates into bribery or the extortion mentioned in this chapter and detailed in Peter Schweizer's books. Mr. Schweizer's proposed solutions [22] (supported by this book) are paraphrased here:

- No Member of Congress can solicit or accept campaign contributions while the US Congress is in session.
- No Member of Congress can solicit or accept campaign contributions from any registered lobbyist or from any government contractor at any time.

So, once they are collected, how are these campaign donations used? Obviously, to fund their campaigns, right?...not so fast.   It is illegal for Members of

Congress to transfer these funds for their own personal use. But they have found creative ways:

- Placing family members on the campaign payroll. [23]
- Loaning their campaign money from their private accounts, and charging high interest rates. [24] [25]
- Shifting funds among Members through the use of Leadership PACs, which have fewer restrictions.

On March 19, 2012, CREW (Citizens for Responsibility and Ethics in Washington) published the 2012 Family Affair report [25], after examining the records of all 435 members of the House. CREW's investigation uncovered 248 members meriting inclusion in this in-depth compilation, which covers the 2008 and 2010 election cycles.

CREW's key findings:

- *82 members (40 Democrats and 42 Republicans) paid family members through their congressional offices, campaign committees and political action committees (PACs);*
- *44 members (20 Democrats and 24 Republicans) have family members who lobby or are employed in government affairs;*

- *90 members (42 Democrats and 48 Republicans) have paid a family business, employer, or associated nonprofit;*
- *20 members (13 Democrats and 7 Republicans) used their campaign money to contribute to a family member's political campaign;*
- *14 members (6 Democrats and 8 Republicans) charged interest on personal loans they made to their own campaigns;*
- *38 members (24 Democrats and 14 Republicans) earmarked to a family business, employer, or associated nonprofit.*

This report marks the first-ever complete study of how members of the House of Representatives use their positions to benefit themselves and their families. Some of the conclusions and recommendations from the CREW report [26] are:

- *Reimbursements for campaign expenses are common and legal, and the expenses are often legitimately related to members' campaigns. Millions of dollars, however, flow through campaign accounts with little oversight and sporadic scrutiny from the toothless FEC, and recently, there have been high profile cases of improper spending.*
- *There is a need to amend the Federal Election Campaign Act (FECA), Federal Election Commission (FEC) regulations, and House rules,*

as well as stronger enforcement of existing rules and regulations.

- *Millions of dollars flow through campaign accounts, and to date, watchdogs and reporters have devoted more time to monitoring donations than disbursements. Given the potential for abuse, changes are needed to make campaign spending more transparent and more easily monitored.*

In addition to this CREW report on the House, a somewhat dated but revealing 2007 National Journal piece gives information on the number of family members as lobbyists, including both the House and Senate: [27]

In what looks like the most authoritative list to date, National Journal reporter Marisa Katz identified 33 Senators and 30 Representatives "who have lobbied or consulted on government relations at the federal or the state level in recent years" in the magazine's March 31, 2007, issue. Regrettably, it doesn't appear that the excellent story that goes with that finding, or the chart, is online at National Journal's site.

Among Senators, Richard Lugar, R-Ind., Mark Pryor, D-Ark., Harry Reid, D-Nev., Pat Roberts, R-Kan., and Ted Stevens, R-Alaska, had a relative with connections, while Rep. Bill Shuster, R-Pa., had two and Rep. Roy Blunt, R-

Mo., was the lone member of Congress to have three.

Since the above report, Roy Blunt has used his power and connections to place family members in strategic positions in both Washington and Missouri politics. His activities, as well as those of Harry Reid and others, are detailed in Chapter 9, "It's a Family Affair" of the book **Extortion**.

Another way in which Members can move money from campaign funds to their personal use is through donating to one another's Leadership PACs. From the CREW 2012 Family Affair report: [28]

> *As the law currently stands, campaign funds may be used to make salary payments to members of a candidate's family only if the family member is providing a bona fide service to the campaign and is paid fair market value. The question of whether a payment constitutes fair market value can be difficult to determine and is rarely challenged. Payments to close family members raise questions of self-dealing, something that could be addressed by prohibiting or limiting the ability of political committees or leadership political action committees (PAC) to make payments to candidates' family members and related businesses and nonprofits. Several states, including Iowa and Louisiana, already prohibit the use of campaign funds to make payments to family members, except in certain cases. In New*

Jersey, candidates are prohibited from paying themselves a salary through their campaign committees, and Texas limits the use of political contributions to make payments to businesses in which the candidate or officeholder has an interest, holds a position in the governing body, or serves as an officer. At the very least, payments to family members should be more transparent. Candidates and their committees should be required to identify recipients of campaign money as family members on their public filings, allowing such payments to be more easily identified and tracked.

From **Extortion**, page 103: [29]

Leadership PACs are ostensibly about raising money to help political colleagues hold and win seats. But the FEC has few restrictions on how these monies can be used and does not restrict the "personal use" of such funds. "Congress has never extended the personal use restrictions to Leadership PACs," says former FEC chairman Michael Toner. "The FEC has looked at this over the years and has determined they don't have the statutory ability to address this. It will take an act of Congress."

How unregulated are these Leadership PACs? Consider the case of Ohio Republican Paul Gillmor's Leadership PAC. During a recent election, PAUL PAC spent almost $6,000 on *personal expenses: fast food, doughnuts, bar tabs, and golf. The problem? Congressman Gillmor was dead. He had tragically fallen down the stairs months earlier. And yet PAUL PAC was picking up the tab for pizza deliveries, visits to Mexican restaurants, Dunkin' Donuts, and more. Intrepid Wall Street Journal reporters Brody Mullens and Brad Haynes uncovered the story and asked the PAC manager about the expenditures. He had a simple explanation: the expenditures were necessary because the PAC members had "gathered many times as we were all grieving to help each other with the job search process." There was apparently nothing illegal about using "grieving funds" to go golfing.*

After considering the information and recommendations from CREW, Peter Schweizer, and other sources, this book supports these reforms:

- Ban Leadership PACs.
- Ban employing family members in the Member's campaign.
- Prohibit the charging of any interest on any loan from a Member to his campaign.

Chapter 6

Insider Trading by Members of Congress

There are a variety of ways that Members of Congress can unethically profit in the stock market by using inside information or power that they have:

- Trading stock (long or short) on information that is in a bill being written or a policy that is being discussed – information that is not yet available to the public.
- Pushing or blocking bills that affect an industry or company that the Member is already invested in.
- Be given permission to invest in IPOs.

The book **Throw Them All Out** describes several examples. Here are some excerpts that involved the sub-prime mortgage financial crisis [30]:

> On Tuesday, September 16, 2008, when Henry Paulson and Fed Chairman Ben Bernanke held another of their terrifying closed-door meetings with congressional leaders (two days before the "ashen-faced" meeting), the stock market had dipped only a few percentage points, and most people assumed that the financial crisis was a disruption that would have just a limited effect

on the broader economy. But what Paulson and Bernanke told lawmakers on September 16 made it clear that the public's perception was wrong. Paulson, in his memoir, explains that during the meeting he outlined that the federal government was going to bail out the insurance giant AIG and that the markets were in deep trouble. "There was almost a surreal quality to the meeting," he recounts. "The stunned lawmakers looked at us as if not quite believing what they were hearing." The next day, Congressman Jim Moran, Democrat of Virginia, a member of the Appropriations Committee, dumped his shares in ninety different companies...

Senator Dick Durbin, the Democratic whip and Chairman of the Sub-Committee on Financial Services and General Government of the Senate Appropriations Committee, attended that September 16 briefing with Paulson and Bernanke. He sold off $73,715 in stock funds the next day. Following the next terrifying closed-door meeting on September 18, he dumped another $42,000 in stock. In doing so, Durbin joined some colleagues in saving themselves from the sizable losses that less connected investors would experience. The stock market collapsed shortly after those congressional trades. By October 3rd, just 17 *days after the September 18 meeting, the market had dropped more than 9%. A month later, it had plummeted over 22%. Preventing a catastrophic loss can be just as important as making a big gain.*

Senator Durbin did not just sell stocks based on his inside knowledge — he was looking for opportunities to invest. Though he had sold many of his holdings, he also bought tens of thousands of dollars' worth of Berkshire Hathaway, the holding company run by the legendary investor Warren Buffett. Durbin bought shares on September 19 and 22 — more than $60,000 worth. His timing was nearly perfect. The next day, September 23, it was announced that Berkshire Hathaway was buying part of Goldman Sachs, which would yield a 10% guaranteed dividend for Berkshire investors like Durbin. The deal had been discussed behind closed doors for days before Buffett announced it publicly. Durbin's spokesman insists that the senator "didn't use any information from that closed-door gathering to counsel his trades the following day. Yet it is almost certain that Durbin, as chairman of a crucial subcommittee, knew about the Goldman Sachs deal...

There are many more well-documented examples of insider trading by Members of Congress in Peter Schweizer's two books.

In 2008 Congress addressed the issue of insider trading by passing the STOCK Act (Stop Trading on Congressional Knowledge). President Barack Obama signed the legislation barring members of Congress, the president and thousands of federal workers from profiting from nonpublic information learned on the job, calling it an embodiment of the fundamental American value of fair play.

Obama said the move to bar insider trading among lawmakers would assure everyone "plays by the same rules."

"It's the notion that the powerful shouldn't get to create one set of rules for themselves and another set of rules for everybody else," Obama said.

"If we expect that to apply to our biggest corporations and our most successful citizens, it certainly should apply to our elected officials," Obama said. [31]

But then a giant loophole was discovered. From CNN: [32]

> *The STOCK Act requires that any trades of $1,000 or more made on or after July 3 have to be reported to the House and Senate within 45*

days. But the House and Senate have two completely different interpretations of that rule. In the Senate, the Ethics Committee released one page of guidelines last month ruling that members and their spouses and dependent children all have to file reports after they make stock or securities trades. But the House Ethics Committee disagreed.

Its 14-page memo notifies House members and aides covered by the law that their spouses and children aren't covered. The Office of Government Ethics, which oversees all federal executive branch employees, sided with the House, informing its employees that their spouses and children don't need to file these periodic reports.

This interpretation of the law in the House made it essentially meaningless.

Then, in April 2013, the law was partially repealed, citing national security concerns. This excerpt from a Forbes article gives details. [33]

Last month the National Academy Of Public Administration submitted to President Obama and Congress its independent review on making the personal financial disclosures of lawmakers, their legislative staffs, and many executive branch officials, available as part of an online searchable database. The online disclosure was part of a law meant to prevent insider trading in the federal government, but the non-profit research group raised stark national security warnings in its review...

NAPA concluded that the online database would result in "negative outcomes to the missions of national security and law enforcement agencies and their staff members," citing national security and law enforcement officials...

The change to the law Congress passed one year ago was seen by some as an underhanded move by lawmakers to gut the legislation. The Stock Act explicitly banned insider trading by government officials and employees—and made their financial transactions more transparent. It was only passed because of tremendous public pressure during election season.

"They used the NAPA report and said 'this is a bad idea let's undo all the disclosure parts of this bill,'" says Lisa Rosenberg, a Washington lobbyist for the Sunlight Foundation. "What we had advocated is if you are really worried about certain categories of jobs then maybe we need to exempt them with carve outs." Adds Rosenberg: "There is a much more targeted way of addressing the security concerns, we are

not dismissive of the security concerns, but putting the information in file cabinets is not fixing the security concerns."...

The most charitable interpretation is that Congress was facing an instant problem because under the Stock Act online posting was to begin on April 15 and alarm bells were being rung. But passing an amendment saying that a big chunk of the transparency provisions of the law shall not take effect means it will now take an act of Congress to narrowly target any transparency fixes. Why didn't lawmakers just delay implementation pending further review? That's what they have already done in the past. It took a 60 Minutes piece in which Steve Kroft confronted Nancy Pelosi about the purchase of Visa stock (note: Kroft did this after interviewing Peter Schweizer) to get them to move the first time. What will it take to get them to act again?

Peter Schweizer gives several examples of Members investing in stock IPOs for corporations over which they have either direct influence through the passage or blocking of legislation, or in which they have insider knowledge. He proposes that Members should not be allowed to trade stock on companies that are overseen by their committees, and shouldn't be allowed to invest in IPOs [34]. This book suggests a simpler and more restrictive law: ban Members from *any* trading in the stock market except by investing in a stock index fund:

No Senator or Representative can own any investment in common stock, preferred stock, bonds of any type, mutual funds, or any other type of investment except as described here: Each Senator or Representative may invest in a fund, similar to an index mutual fund, representing a broad offering of investments, to be created for this purpose. Between the times that the Senator or Representative is elected/re-elected and sworn in, he will sell all stocks, bonds, etc. that he owns. The Senator or Representative may then invest in the above index fund and may increase or decrease the investment in this index fund while in office. No Senator or Representative can purchase or sell, or influence the purchase or sale, of any stock, bond, or any other investment, except as described above, while in office. This law also applies to the Member's immediate family. This ruling applies only to stocks, bonds, and the like. It does not apply to real estate, ownership or partial ownership in private companies, or other assets. One model that could be considered in structuring this fund would be to offer the same categories of investments that are now offered to federal employees through the well regarded TSP (Thrift Savings Plan):

- Government securities
- Government, corporate, and mortgage-backed bonds
- Stocks of large and medium-sized U.S. companies
- Stocks of small to medium-sized U.S. companies
- International stocks of 22 developed countries

The investor can invest in any category or categories and can change the allocations at any time without penalty. This fund, or one similar to it, represents a sound investment vehicle and is typical of the investments that most Americans have (those who are fortunate to be able to invest at all). It is good enough for Members of Congress as well.

Of course, many Members would strongly object to this reform, calling it extreme, unnecessary, and unfair. It isn't. If a particular Member or candidate considers his stock investments to be a higher priority than his congressional duties, no problem....he doesn't have to run. We have lots of good potential candidates. This is a reasonable, sensible reform to discourage the practice of insider trading. In addition, this reform would eliminate the issue (if it is even a valid concern) of "negative outcomes to the missions of national security and law enforcement agencies and their staff members," resulting from the disclosure and transparency aspects of the STOCK Act, cited earlier in this chapter.

Chapter 7

Ethics Committees – A Good Concept; Let's Improve On It

Each of the houses of Congress has an Ethics Committee, with laws and rules on ethical behavior and official codes of conduct. But it is evident that few Americans are of the opinion that these committees are fully doing their jobs. In 2008, as an additional safeguard, the US House of Representatives established the Office of Congressional Ethics (OCE), charged with reviewing allegations of misconduct against members of the House of Representatives and their staff and, when appropriate, referring matters to the United States House Committee on Standards of Official Conduct, commonly referred to as the Ethics Committee. This was a step in the right direction, and the OCE has received favorable reports on doing its job. From the Washington Times, March 29, 2012: [35]

> *Some members have pushed back hard against the new ethics investigators, bitterly complaining about their tactics, and have even led unsuccessful efforts to slash the office's funding. But watchdogs argue the office has helped shine a bright light of transparency and accountability on the House ethics process,*

which was previously cloaked in secrecy, fraught with politics and had too often become a black hole where allegations against members went to die...

Despite these limitations, the office has conducted more investigations in three years than the full committee has in more than a decade, sending 29 public referrals to the Ethics Committee for future action.

Melanie Sloan, Executive Director of CREW, explained the extent of corruption in Congress and the limited power given to the OCE to deal with it in an excellent October 13, 2010 posting. Here is an excerpt: [36]

There is no better way to make the case for increased ethics enforcement, than by highlighting the deplorable conduct of lawmakers who belong to an institution that refuses to police itself. Their actions run the gamut from bribery, to using their office for personal gain, to solicitation of prostitution. Sadly, many of these members of Congress will never have to answer for their misdeeds.

As it stands now, the OCE has no subpoena power and a very limited time frame to investigate any allegations of wrongdoing. What's more is that it can only look at misconduct that has occurred since March 2008. In spite of being forced to fight with one hand tied behind its back, the OCE has referred

13 cases to the House Ethics Committee for review, though the committee has taken action against only two. Even that limited success has brought the OCE powerful enemies, prompting members of both parties to openly talk of stripping away the OCE's authority -- or even dismantling the office altogether -- in the 112th Congress. Congresswoman Marcia Fudge (D-OH) has proposed legislation that would eviscerate the OCE, and Minority Leader John Boehner (R-OH) has said he wants to "take a look" at its usefulness.

Meanwhile, the Senate has nothing comparable to the OCE, but clearly needs one. The Senate Ethics Committee has allowed Sen. David Vitter (R-LA) to skate for years, barely commented when former Sen. Pete Domenici (R-NM) tried to push a U.S. Attorney to conduct a criminal investigation for political purposes, and blamed itself when Sens. Kent Conrad (D-ND) and Chris Dodd (D-CT) received preferential treatment from Countrywide Financial. Further, it has yet to utter a peep in response to Sen. John Ensign's (R-NV) thoroughly reprehensible and despicable conduct.

It's clear that the House and the Senate have both done a dismal job of policing the conduct of their members. While Congressman Charles Rangel (D-NY) and Congresswoman Maxine Waters (D-CA) are scheduled to face ethics hearings for their actions next month, there may not be any future ethics enforcement if OCE is kneecapped, or worse, eliminated.

Ethics isn't about Republican or Democrat; it's about right and wrong. Both houses of Congress and both political parties have a less-than-stellar record on this issue. The American people deserve a Congress free of ethically challenged people. The best way to make that happen is to ensure there are strong, independent ethics offices keeping an eye on our supposedly "honorable" elected officials.

This important flaw in limiting the authority and power of the OCE is further explained in this excerpt from a Roll Call article dated March 18, 2013: [37]

The role of the OCE is quite limited, which is unfortunate. As formulated by the House rules, the OCE acts as the independent office that serves as an entry point for allegations of ethics violations by House members and their staffs. Through its fact-finding, the OCE determines whether an allegation should be dismissed, or whether there is sufficient reason for the Ethics Committee to undertake further investigation. It has no power to compel testimony or to make any determination of guilt or innocence. In sum, it acts as a screening mechanism to sift out the legitimate concerns from the frivolous or incorrect. Its role is somewhat similar to, though far weaker than, a grand jury in that its role is to determine whether the allegations brought forward merit being sent on for further action.

Of course, that is not the role that the OCE should be playing. The OCE should have subpoena authority and should act as the investigatory arm for the ethics process while the Ethics Committee should serve the adjudicatory function. As it is, there is needless duplication in the process.

The OCE is comprised of eight board members and a staff of nine. It has two Co-Chairs, David Skaggs and Peter Goss.

David Skaggs was executive director of the Center for Democracy & Citizenship at the Council for Excellence in Government and Of Counsel to the Washington-based law firm, Hogan & Hartson. He also served as an Adjunct Professor at the University of Colorado (1999-2002). These positions followed twelve years in Congress (1987-99) as U.S. Representative from the 2nd Congressional District of Colorado (the northwestern Denver suburbs) and three terms in the

Colorado House (1981-87), the last two terms as Minority Leader.

Peter Goss served in Congress for 16 years until his appointment by President George W. Bush to be Director of the Central Intelligence Agency (CIA). While in the House, Goss served as chair of the House Intelligence Committee from 1997 until 2005 and the vice-chairman of the House Rules Committee.

Five of the other six board members are former Member of the US House of Representatives. The sixth, Jay Eagen, served as Chief Administrative Officer of the United States House of Representatives in the 105th, 106th, 107th, 108th, 109th and 110th Congresses. He served as Chief Administrative Officer Emeritus in 2007 until his retirement in May of that year.

Nothing against this group; they seem to be doing their job well. But, did you notice, they are all card-carrying members of Washington's Permanent Political Class! Wouldn't the cause of maintaining ethical standards be well served with a board of highly-qualified individuals from OUTSIDE Washington?

A proposed improvement: Reorganize the OCE to accomplish all duties, except adjudication, currently accomplished by both the United States House Committee on Standards of Official Conduct and the OCE. Increase the OCE staffing to 16 board members and 20 staff. Shrink the United States House Committee on Standards of Official Conduct to two Representatives and four staff, who will have, along with the Speaker of the House and the Minority Leader, the duty to adjudicate any violations of official conduct. The representatives will also select OCE board members for four year terms, on a rotating basis. Every two years, prior to the start of each Congressional session, the four above representatives would select eight members for the OCE board from a list of nominees provided by the governors of each of the fifty states, on a rotating basis. No person who has served as a Member of Congress (either House), as a registered lobbyist, or as a cabinet secretary in the executive branch would be allowed to serve on the OCE board. Each of the current members of the OCE will complete their current terms to provide a smooth transition.

The US Senate does not currently have an entity comparable to the OCE in the House, and it certainly needs one. Some insight into the performance of the US Senate Select Committee on Ethics is provided in a January 3, 2014 blog from CREW. [38] It details some of their efforts over the past ten years in filing ethics complaints against Members of the Senate. An excerpt is below:

> *Since CREW began operating in 2003, we have filed ethics complaints against 21 senators and*

one Senate staff member. Most of these matters dragged on for years, and the committee frequently failed to respond in any way.

For instance, the committee ignored complaints against then-Sens. Rick Santorum (R-PA) and Norm Coleman (R-MN) for accepting improper gifts and a complaint against then-Sen. Kit Bond (R-MO) for improperly pressuring the White House to remove a U.S. Attorney due to a disagreement the senator had with the U.S. attorney's brother.

When the committee has responded to CREW, it has rarely held members accountable for misconduct, often waving off serious allegations based on technicalities. After CREW filed complaints against then-Senate Majority Leader Bill Frist (R-TN) over insider-trading allegations in 2005, the committee waited until January 2007 before writing that it no longer had jurisdiction in the matter because Sen. Frist had retired. After Sen. David Vitter's (R-LA) phone number appeared on the call list of a D.C. madam, the committee dismissed our complaint alleging that solicitation of prostitutes did not reflect creditably on the Senate because the alleged misconduct took place while Sen. Vitter was in the House, not the Senate.

The committee dismissed our complaints against Sen. Chris Dodd (D-CT) and Kent Conrad

(D-ND) for improperly accepting favorable terms on their mortgages as part of the Countrywide scandal, explaining that the Senate rules prohibiting these special benefits were not spelled out clearly enough — a rationale so ludicrous CREW floated Battered Committee Syndrome as a possible explanation for the panel's failure to act.

It is proposed that an entity be established in the Senate with the same duties and responsibilities as described above for the reorganized OCE. Current and proposed staffing for both Houses is shown on the following page:

United States House Committee on Standards of Official Conduct		
	Current Members	
Board Members	10	Representatives - 5 Democrats and 5 Republicans
Staff	25	
House Office of Congressional Ethics		
Board Members	8	Private Citizens
Staff	9	
	Proposed Members	
Board Members	4	Representatives - 2 Democrats and 2 Republicans
Staff	4	
House Office of Congressional Ethics		
Board Members	16	Private Citizens
Staff	20	

United States Senate Select Committee on Ethics		
	Current Members	
Board Members	6	Senators - 3 Democrats and 3 Republicans
Staff	12	
Senate Office of Congressional Ethics		No office currently exists for the US Senate.
Board Members		
Staff		
	Proposed Members	
Board Members	2	Senators - 1 Democrat and 1 Republican
Staff	2	
Senate Office of Congressional Ethics		
Board Members	8	Private Citizens
Staff	6	

Chapter 8

Needed: An Informed, Engaged, Open-Minded Citizenry

The reforms offered in this book and elsewhere can only be accomplished by the US Congress itself, due to the separation of powers clause in the Constitution. It will not be an easy task to persuade the current Members of Congress to initiate any of these reforms, since the current system provides them significant advantages over their challengers in elections and because the current system is rife with unethical practices that can make them rich. The Members are apparently not going to consider making improvements that would provide a more enduring and just system, because few of them are going to look beyond the next election.

Furthermore, in contrast to the usual partisan confrontation on most matters of public policy, the Democrats and Republicans are completely in agreement in their opposition to any of these reforms. They are in lock-step in ignoring and dismissing any calls (and there have been many) to eliminate their unethical behavior.

So, the initiatives must start with us, the citizens. We must develop and collaborate on proposed reforms and promulgate them to each Member of Congress. We must elect (or re-elect) only those who are prepared to step up and assist in this effort.

If we are too focused on particular agendas, or in being stalwart participants in the struggle between liberals and conservatives, or if we are simply apathetic, nothing will change. When Members of Congress talk to us using demagoguery, partisan hype, and over-simplistic answers, they are of course hoping for our support and our money. But are they also distracting us? Maybe we are being played a little:

Let's go to the game! Yay, (Democrats, Republicans, liberals, conservatives, progressives, libertarians...)! Let's slam the opponents and gripe about the calls from the officials (courts)! Let's have a good time! But, uh...pay no attention to that group quietly moving through the stands picking everyone's pockets.

In the matter of the behavior of our Members of the US Congress, we need to concentrate a little less on what is right or left, and instead focus more on what is right and wrong.

So, what can an individual American do about any of this? Here are some (rather obvious) suggestions:

- Voting is good; being an informed voter is even better.

- Put some time into studying the issues that are important to you. Be passionate, open-minded, receptive, and proactive in presenting your views.

- If you are interested in any of the issues described or referenced in this book, take a critical look at the proposed solutions and offer comments or improvements.

- Don't limit yourself to these issues. There are certainly other important issues involving Congress that are not discussed in this short book. For example, a Member is appointed to a congressional committee not based upon experience, knowledge, or even seniority, but simply based upon the amount of dues that Member pays to the party. [39] The books and websites referenced here offer many more examples and perspectives on congressional corruption than are included here.

- You may want to get involved in an organization. Certainly there are many good organizations and individuals trying to address these issues. Some are referenced in this book. We should all recognize and be grateful for the efforts made by watchdog groups and news organizations such as Citizens for Responsibility and Ethics in Washington (CREW), Citizens Against Government Waste (CAGW), the Government Accountability Institute, Roll Call,

Common Cause, The CATO Institute, the Sunlight Foundation, The Hill, Taxpayers for Common Sense, and others for their diligent efforts. These groups (some left leaning, some right leaning; nothing wrong with that) share a commitment to expose ethical issues in Congress and to seek solutions.

- A copy of this book has been sent to each US Representative and Senator, with the request that they consider these reforms. Each is invited to respond by email, US mail, or through a website. I don't expect much in response. If you are interested in any of this, you are also invited to respond. **Better yet, make your opinions known to your Senators or Representative. They are more likely to respond to a constituent in their state or district than to me.**

- The website offers more resources and suggestions on actions that you can take.

- Remember this: when it comes to representative democracy, our nation has a very strong bench. Consider the people that you know: most are honest Americans of good will. Of these, at least a few of them (say, 5%, 1 out of 20) are individuals with impressive character and accomplishments, who are certainly capable of being good Members of the US Congress. There are about 182 million

Americans over the age of 30 (the minimum age for the Senate; the House minimum age is 25). Five percent of those is about 9,100,000 highly qualified potential candidates, or about 17,000 for each one of the 535 congressional seats. Of course this rough estimate doesn't take into account variations among states and districts, but you get the idea. These incumbents are not indispensable. Why don't you run for office, or give your strong support to someone who is?

Website: www.atimeforintegrity.com

Email: info@atimeforintegrity.com

US Mail: A Time for Integrity
            P. O. Box 69171
            Oro Valley, AZ 85737

Chapter 9

A Yearning for Integrity

Our Federal Government must be able to govern better than it does now.

On most public policy issues, there are reasonable perspectives and principles to support various arguments and solutions. But our US Congress will not be able to govern effectively, find common ground, and make progress on these issues until each Member starts behaving in a more responsible and ethical manner.

The purpose of our US Congress is to have sincere, spirited analysis and debate on matters of public policy, followed by voting based on individual judgments, priorities, and values, in keeping with American principles and Constitutional law.

Its purpose is not for its Members to buy and sell votes, extort money from the private sector, engage in insider trading, place party loyalty above all principles, find ways to become rich through larceny, and threaten anyone who objects to these activities.

These practices are not the result of group failures. Group pressure and influence are certainly primary causes of these failures, but these are individual failures. Good or bad character is an individual trait.

They need to stop using rationalizations to justify their behavior:

- It's legal. (As previously noted, it is only legal because they make the laws.)
- Everyone is doing it.
- I must do it to be effective for the constituents of my state or district.
- I must do it to be effective in supporting my party.
- I must do it to be effective in supporting liberal / conservative agendas.

All of these rationalizations have one thing in common. They are all unacceptable in trying to justify unethical behavior.

Of course, some Members engage in these unethical practices much less than others. That may be commendable, but it is not enough. Each Member in both Houses of the Legislature should be condemning these practices and working continually to eliminate them.

Each Member must value an ethical Congress more highly than he values his own re-election.

One irony here is that although every Member of Congress craves power, they actually are not accepting the power that is vested in them:

- They have the power and responsibility to create an annual budget, but haven't created one in five years. Instead, the federal government staggers along through the use of a series of continuing resolutions. These are based upon flimsy financial baselines, deliberately misleading projections, insincere estimates, questionable accounting, and not much control by Congress. The result is that the President pretty much spends however much he wants on whatever he wants. In a recent interview with Greta Van Susteren on Fox News regarding the federal budget, Congressman Paul Ryan (R-WI) said "We are supposed to set spending; we are supposed to prioritize funding; we are supposed to exercise the power of the purse. For the last three years, we have been doing these things called continuing resolutions, where we delegate that power to the executive branch. So, I want Congress to reclaim that power from the administration." [40]
- It is widely accepted that annual deficits of federal government spending, causing ever increasing national debt, cannot be sustained, and for these deficits to be reduced and

eventually eliminated, there must be a balance between spending and tax revenues. Solving this compelling issue is the responsibility of Congress, not the Executive Branch! But neither party in Congress will pursue a solution with any vigor, because each party fears political ramifications more than it fears for our nation's fiscal stability.

- We want Congress to have detailed, sincere, informed, comprehensive, open-minded debates on the issues of the day, and we citizens would like to hear some of them. But what we get is:
  o Almost-empty speeches to almost-empty chambers on C-SPAN.
  o Very brief sound bites and talking points on the Sunday shows.
  o Campaign speeches in front of partisan crowds, featuring blame, demagoguery, simplistic statements, and often lies.
  o Franked mailings of campaign literature ill-disguised as news.
- In addition, Congress has a Constitutional duty and responsibility to conduct oversight on the Executive Branch, but it will likely not be effective in this until it improves its own ethical standards.

Why aren't they doing any of this? One reason is that an estimated 30% to 70% of each Member's day is spent on fund-raising. [41] Other activities discussed in this book (setting earmarks, insider trading, campaigning, travelling between their home state and Washington, DC, etc.) also take time.

We want our Members of Congress to face the compelling issues of the day. Instead, they are playing small ball.

Chapter 10

Proposed Reforms

The following is a list of proposed reforms, with brief comments supporting each:

1. No Senator or Representative can solicit or accept campaign contributions while the US Congress is in session. **Comment:** This will provide more separation, in time and space, between contributions and the writing of legislation, and will give Members more time to meet their legislative responsibilities.

2. No Senator or Representative can solicit or accept campaign contributions from any registered lobbyist or from any government contractor at any time. **Comment:** Lobbyists, government contractors, etc., can still make their views known to Congress, but this reform would reduce the amount of bribery and extortion now occurring.

3. No family member of any Senator or Representative can be a registered lobbyist. **Comment:** This is an obvious conflict of interest.

4. No family member of any Senator or Representative can be a paid employee of the

Senator or Representative's campaign. **Comment:** This practice is often simply a method to transfer funds from the campaign to the Member's personal use.

5. Leadership PACs are banned. **Comment:** Leadership PACs have few restrictions and have become ways to move campaign funds among Members for their personal use.

6. The ban on earmarks is permanent. **Comment:** Member's votes must be based upon their position on the primary subject of the bill, not on an unrelated side deal through an earmark.

7. Each bill will be focused on one specific subject. No part of the bill will be about an unrelated subject or unrelated funding. **Comment:** This will further prevent the practice of inserting earmarks or other unrelated funding into a bill.

8. The Obama administration will complete its efforts to make letter-marking requests available to the public in a searchable database. **Comment:** Disclosure of these requests can be a deterrent in some cases, and will provide transparency on this inappropriate practice.

9. The ethics rules in both houses of Congress will require more detailed and timely information on both the receiving and disbursement of campaign funds by each Member. **Comment:** The current standards on reporting are too lax, and often even those standards are not met.

10. In addition to the rules and constraints currently in place regarding redistricting, state legislatures will be required to meet an empirical standard on "compactness." One suggested model is presented in this book. **Comment:** This requirement will greatly reduce the ability of incumbents to essentially select their voters through extreme gerrymandering of the district boundaries. This is the only reform in this list that would require a constitutional amendment. That can be accomplished by a supermajority of two-thirds of both houses of Congress, and then ratification by three-fourths of the states.

11. Prior to a vote on any bill, it will be available on line, in its final form, for a minimum of seven days. It will be accompanied with two summaries of the bill (in 1,000 words or fewer), one provided by each of the two major parties. These summaries will not be legal or binding in nature, but will give each major party an opportunity to briefly present to the public its interpretation of the major elements of the bill and its general position on that bill. **Comment:** This would allow various factions and interest groups, as well as the public at large, to see and respond to a bill before it is voted upon.

12. No Senator or Representative can own any investment in common stock, preferred stock, bonds of any type, mutual funds, or any other

type of investment except as described here: Each Senator or Representative may invest in a fund, similar to an index mutual fund, representing a broad offering of investments, to be created for this purpose, as described in Chapter 6. Between the times that the Senator or Representative is elected/re-elected and sworn in, he will sell all stocks, bonds, etc. The Senator or Representative may then invest in the above index fund and may increase or decrease the investment in this index fund while in office. No Senator or Representative can purchase or sell, or influence the purchase or sale, of any stock, bond, or any other investment, except as described above, while in office. This law also applies to the Member's immediate family. This ruling applies only to stocks, bonds, and the like. It does not apply to real estate, ownership or partial ownership in private companies, or other assets. **Comment:** This is a reasonable, sensible reform to discourage the practice of insider trading. In addition, it will give Members more time to conduct their congressional duties, and will eliminate any national security issues regarding disclosure.

13. No Senator or Representative can provide information to any person or entity that will result in that person or entity having an advantage in buying or selling any type of

investment, unless that information is already fully available to the public. **Comment:** This is a further attempt to prevent or discourage insider trading.

14. If a Senator or Representative loans money to his or her campaign, he or she cannot collect any interest on that loan. **Comment:** Members often use loans at high interest rates to move funds from their campaigns to their personal use. A current rule specifies the use of "market rates", but it is rarely enforced and violations are frequent.

15. "Whistleblower" laws, which have already been applied to the US Executive Branch and to the private sector, now apply to the US Congress. **Comment:** We certainly need whistleblower laws to apply to Members of Congress and their staffs, probably more than anywhere else.

16. Congress will be subjected to the Freedom of Information Act, just as the Executive Branch is. **Comment:** All of the unethical practices described or referenced in this book are exacerbated by the lack of transparency in Congress.

17. (For the US House only): The United States House Committee on Standards of Official Conduct and the Office of Congressional Ethics (OCE) will be reorganized. The OCE will accomplish all duties, except adjudication, currently accomplished by both the United

States House Committee on Standards of Official Conduct and the OCE. The OCE staffing will be increased to 16 board members and 20 staff. The United States House Committee on Standards of Official Conduct will be comprised of two Representatives and four staff, and will have, along with the Speaker of the House and the Minority Leader, the duty to adjudicate any violations of official conduct. OCE board members will be selected for four year terms, on a rotating basis. Every two years, prior to the start of each Congressional session, the four above Representatives will select eight members for the OCE board from a list of nominees provided by the governors of each of the fifty states. No person who has served as a Member of Congress (either House), a registered lobbyist, or a cabinet secretary in the executive branch can serve on the OCE board. **Comment:** A strong, powerful, objective, rigorous board is needed to enforce the ethics rules of the House and to strengthen those rules as needed.

18. (For the US Senate only): An Office of Ethics of the US Senate (OES) will be established, which will be somewhat comparable to the OCE in the US House of Representatives. The OES will accomplish all duties, except adjudication, currently accomplished by the United States Senate Select Committee on Ethics. The OES

will be comprised of eight board members and six staff. The United States Senate Select Committee on Ethics will be comprised of two Senators and two staff, and will have, along with the Senate Majority Leader and the Senate Minority Leader, the duty to adjudicate any violations of official conduct. OES board members will be selected for four year terms, on a rotating basis. Every two years, prior to the start of each Congressional session, the four above Senators will select four members for the OES board from a list of nominees provided by the governors of each of the fifty states. No person who has served as a Member of Congress (either House), a registered lobbyist, or a cabinet secretary in the executive branch can serve on the OES board. **Comment:** A strong, powerful, objective, rigorous board is needed to enforce the ethics rules of the Senate and to strengthen those rules as needed.

Chapter 11

A Challenge and an Opportunity for Each

Member of Congress

Here is a simple question directed to each Member of Congress:

Will you work to make our Congress more ethical and more productive?

I challenge you to either pledge to support each of these reforms or to explain why you won't.

I am requesting a response.

> Website: www.atimeforintegrity.com

> Email: info@atimeforintegrity.com

> US Mail: A Time for Integrity
>   P. O. Box 69171
>   Oro Valley, AZ 85737

All responses will be made publically available on the website.

From the Introduction of the book **Extortion**: [40]

" *No wonder that a large portion of the American people distrust the federal government, regardless of who is in power. According to Pew Research, only 30% of the American people trust the federal government. This also explains why Transparency International, an international organization that tracks "perceptions of corruption" in countries around the world, has the United States well below Singapore and Barbados on its "corruption perception index". Meanwhile, Washington DC and the Permanent Political Class" prosper.*

The numbers are startling. The World Bank scores what it calls "worldwide governance indicators" and measures each country's "control of corruption". In recent years, the United States has continued to slip in the rankings. Since 2009, the United States has dropped to the very bottom of developed countries in that category. The World Economic Forum has created a similar scale as part of its Global Competitiveness Report. Here, too, the United States scores below most other developed countries when it comes to dealing with corruption.

What happens in Washington doesn't stay in Washington. It undermines the entire country.

Is it any wonder that the Italian Mafia was initially developed in Sicily – by politicians?"

The reforms discussed here would significantly change the way Congress works, and the way Washington works. Many would say that it is simply naïve to suggest or hope that any of them would take place.

But, instead, it may be naïve of the Members of Congress to assume that the American public will continue to tolerate their behavior. It is time for a change.

The human race has a real opportunity during the next 100 – 200 years. It can become freer, healthier, more enlightened, more secure, more peaceful, more prosperous, and more fulfilling. Or it can sink into darkness. Of all the factors that will determine this outcome, the most important one is whether the nations of the world will have good governments, or corrupt ones.

What role will our nation play?

NOTES

1. Greg Giroux, "Voters Throw Bums *In* While Holding Congress in Disdain", *Bloomberg News*, December 12, 2012

2. *University of Virginia Center for Politics*, "Sabato's Crystal Ball", updated December 9, 2013 http://www.centerforpolitics.org/crystalball/articles/category/2014-house/

3. Mark Leibovich, *This Town* Blue Rider Press (Penguin Group, 2013), page 163

4. Ibid, pages 164-166

5. Peter Schweizer, *Throw Them All Out* (Houghton Mifflin Harcourt, 2011), page 158

6. Peter Schweizer, *Throw Them All Out* (Houghton Mifflin Harcourt, 2011)

7. "Family Affair, 2012 Edition", Citizens for Responsibility and Ethics in Washington (CREW), http://www.citizensforethics.org/

8. Chris Unger, "Why Congress Cannot Operate Without The Bribing Power Of Earmarks", *Forbes*, December 29, 2012, http://www.forbes.com/sites/rickungar/2012/12/29/why-congress-cannot-operate-without-the-bribing-power-of-earmarks /

9. Humberto Sanchez, *Are Earmarks Really Dead?*, Roll Call, November 26, 2012, http://www.rollcall.com/news/are_earmarks_really_dead-219368-1.html

10. Kevin Bogardus, "Obama administration draft memo could shed light on 'letter-marking'", The Hill, November 9, 2011, http://thehill.com/business-a-lobbying/192497-obama-administration-draft-memo-could-shed-light-on-lettermarking

11. Marlys Harris, "Are 'letter-marks' Congress' new end-around on the earmarks ban?", Minnpost.com, September 20, 2013

12. Scott A. Frisch and Sean Q. Kelly, *Cheese Factories on the Moon – Why Earmarks Are Good for American Democracy,* (Paradigm Publishers, 2011), Preface

13. Ibid, page 62

14. CREW report (Citizens for Responsibility and Ethics in Washington; Top Scandals of 2012), http://www.citizensforethics.org/

15. Peter Schweizer, *Extortion* (Houghton Mifflin Harcourt, 2013), page 178

16. Brennan Center for Justice, "7 Things to Know About Redistricting" October 28, 2013 http://www.brennancenter.org/analysis/7-things-know-about-redistricting

17. Patrick Basham and Dennis Polhill, The CATO Institute, Policy Analysis Number 547, June 30, 2005, "Uncompetitive Elections and the American Political System"

http://www.cato.org/publications/policy-analysis/uncompetitive-elections-american-political-system

18. Lois Beckett, ProPublica, "Is Partisan Gerrymandering Unconstitutional?" November 7, 2011 http://www.propublica.org/article/is-partisan-gerrymandering-unconstitutional

19. Peter Schweizer, *Extortion* (Houghton Mifflin Harcourt, 2013), pages 12 -13

20. Ibid, pages 59-61

21. Lawrence Lessig, Daily Beast, "Congressmen Come And Go, But Corruption Is Here To Stay", June 7, 2013

22. Peter Schweizer, *Extortion* (Houghton Mifflin Harcourt, 2013), pages 175-177

23. Ibid, pages 151-170

24. Ibid, page 74

25. "Family Affair, 2012 Edition", Citizens for Responsibility and Ethics in Washington (CREW), http://www.citizensforethics.org/

26. Ibid

27. Bill Allison, Sunlight Foundation, "National Journal: 63 Current Members of Congress Have Relatives with Ties to Lobbying", April 9, 2007

28. "Family Affair, 2012 Edition", Citizens for Responsibility and Ethics in Washington (CREW), http://www.citizensforethics.org/

29. Peter Schweizer, *Extortion* (Houghton Mifflin Harcourt, 2013), page 103

30. Peter Schweizer, *Throw Them All Out* (Houghton Mifflin Harcourt, 2011), pages 32-35

31. The Associated Press, "Obama Signs STOCK Act Into Law", April 4, 2012

32. Deirdre Walsh and Dana Bash, CNN, ""CNN exclusive: Congressional insider trading ban might not apply to families", July 19, 2012

33. Nathan Vardi, Forbes, "Did Obama And Congress Use National Security Fears To Gut The Stock Act?", April 21, 2013

34. Peter Schweizer, *Throw Them All Out* (Houghton Mifflin Harcourt, 2011),   pages 174-175

35. Susan Crabtree, "Small office has big job as monitor of ethics in the House", The Washington Times, March 19, 2012

36. Melanie Sloan, Executive Director, Citizens for Responsibility and Ethics in Washington (CREW), October 13, 2010, http://www.citizensforethics.org/

37. Meredith McGehee, "Office of Congressional Ethics is a Singular Success" Roll Call, March 18, 2013

38. CREW Staff Blog, "Sudden Outbreak of Productivity in the Senate Ethics Committee", January 4, 2014 http://www.citizensforethics.org/blog/entry/sudden-outbreak-of-productivity-in-senate-ethics-committee-mitch-mcconnell

39. Peter Schweizer, *Extortion* (Houghton Mifflin Harcourt, 2013), pages 63-68

40. "On the Record with Greta Van Susteren", Fox News, December 10, 2013 http://video.foxnews.com/v/2920917120001/rep-paul-ryan-breaks-down-tentative-budget-deal/

41. Peter Schweizer, *Extortion* (Houghton Mifflin Harcourt, 2013), page 58

42. Peter Schweizer, *Extortion* (Houghton Mifflin Harcourt, 2013), Page 20

Index

Pryor, Mark	59			
Public Citizen	21			
Rangel, Charles	74			
Reid, Harry	59	60		
Roberts, Pat	59			
Roll Call	16	75	85	
Rosenberg, Lisa	68			
Ryan, Paul	90			
Sanchez, Humberto	16			
Santorum, Rick	79			
Schweizer, Peter	5	7	31	50	56
	66	69		
Shuster, Bill	59			
Sixty Minutes	69			
Skaggs, David	76			
Sloan, Melanie	73			
Stevens, Ted	59			
Sunlight Foundation	68	86		
Taxpayers for Common Sense	18	22	86	
The Cato Institute	35	86		
The Hill	17	18	24	86
This Town	7			
Throw Them All Out	5	12	63	
Toner, Michael	61			
Ungar, Rick	14	16		
University of Virginia Center for Politics	4			
US Supreme Court	43			
Van Susteren, Greta	90			
Vitter, David	74	79		
Wall Street Journal	62			
Washington Post	9			
Washington Times	72			
Waters, Maxine	74			

www.ingramcontent.com/pod-product-compliance
Lightning Source LLC
Chambersburg PA
CBHW060413290526
45791CB00002B/729